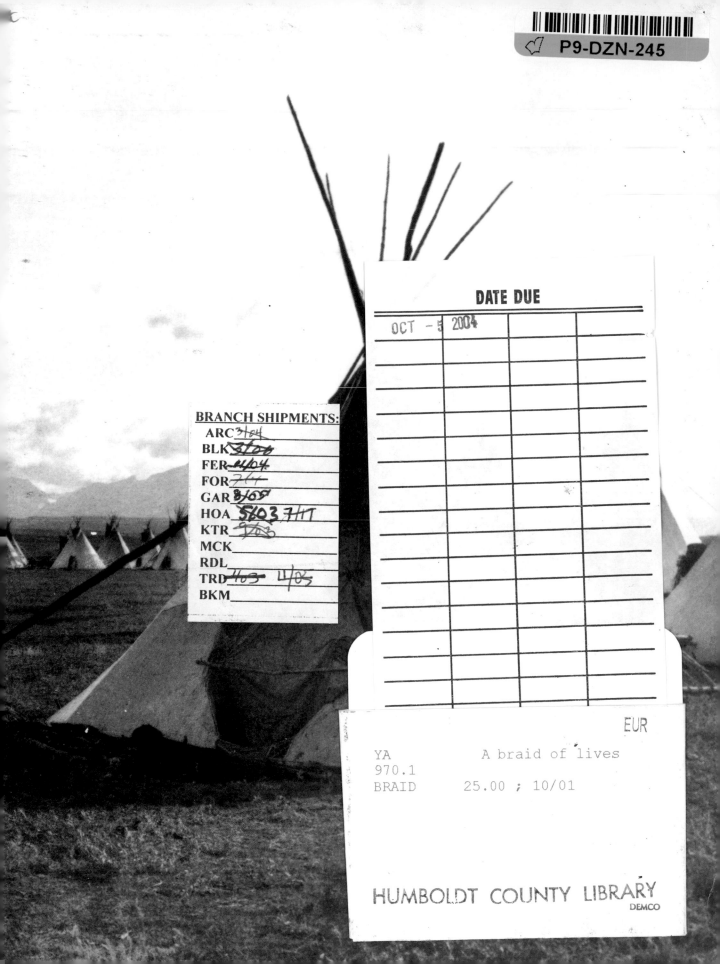

# A BRAID OF LIVES

# A BRAID OF LIVES

## Native American Childhood

EDITED BY NEIL PHILIP

CLARION BOOKS

NEW YORK

For Sue Kimm
and Seymour Grufferman

Clarion Books
a Houghton Mifflin Company imprint
215 Park Avenue South, New York, NY 10003

Published in the United States in 2000 by arrangement with
The Albion Press Ltd, Spring Hill, Idbury, Oxfordshire OX7 6RU, England

Library of Congress Cataloging-in-Publication Data

A braid of lives : Native American childhood / edited by Neil Philip.
      p. cm.
   Includes bibliographical references.
   Summary: weaves the testimony of many Native Americans into a single narrative of
childhood and growing up.
   ISBN 0-395-64528-X
   1. Indian children—Biography—Juvenile literature. 2. Indians of North
America—Biography—Juvenile literature. 3. Indian philosophy—North America—Juvenile
literature. [1. Indians of North America—Biography.] I. Philip, Neil.

E98.C5 B73 2000
973'.0497'00922—dc21
   [B]                                              00-021343

Design: Emma Bradford

Typesetting by York House Typographic, London
Printed in Hong Kong/China by South China Printing Co.

10 9 8 7 6 5 4 3 2 1

ENDPAPERS: Edward S. Curtis *Piegan encampment* Piegan 1900
HALF-TITLE PAGE: Edward S. Curtis *Playmates* Crow 1905 (detail)
FACING TITLE PAGE: Richard Throssel *Crow camp* Crow 1910 (detail)

# INTRODUCTION

When in 1909 the photographer Joseph Kossuth Dixon asked the Blackfoot warrior Mountain Chief for "a story of his boyhood days," the old man refused. He wanted to tell tales of hunting and fighting, which he acted out with gusto: "First he is whistling, again he is singing, then he is on his hands and knees on the ground pawing up the dust like a buffalo when he is angry. His gestures are violent and his speech is guttural, like the sputtering of water from an exhaust. He sings a war song of his own composition and you can hear him for a mile."

Eventually the two men compromised, with the lively tale of how the young Mountain Chief learned to trap foxes—a childhood memory to the listener, but for the speaker more truly the first proof of adulthood. This wish to be numbered among the grownups is very clearly stated in many Native American life stories. "I tried to be like my mother," says the Crow medicine woman Pretty-shield. Ohiyesa, a Wahpeton Sioux who as Charles A. Eastman was one of the first truly successful Native American authors, remembers envying the warrior's eagle feathers from infancy—so much so that at the age of two he took his uncle's treasured war bonnet and plucked out its feathers for himself.

So while Native American autobiographies tell of many things familiar to us all—love and punishment from parents and grandparents, childhood pranks, and communal games—they do so from a point of view that longs to be an adult rather than yearns to remain a child. Time and again they record how the speaker as a boy or girl was pushed to develop the stamina, strength, and endurance he or she would need as an adult; how proud the boys were of their first hunting successes and the girls of their burgeoning household skills.

But life was not all hard training for adulthood. One constant in the varied cultures of the Indian nations is love of children—indulgence when they are small, and deep concern for their welfare as they grow. It is beautifully expressed in the Navajo prayer for the moment when a child is finally removed from the cradle board, as collected by Louisa Wade Wetherill and published in *Children of the People*, Dorothea Leighton and Clyde Kluckhohn's 1947 study of Navajo individuality. The prayer can be simply modified for a girl rather than a boy, and runs:

Dawn Boy, this is Changing Woman's son
Let him arise with much wealth, many robes
Let him arise with many jewels
This is the earthly son of Changing Woman
With the strength of the earth
With earth's black flint shoes for his moccasins
Let him arise
Let him be draped with the black flint of the earth
Let him be draped with the strength of the earth
Let his hat be made of earth's black flint strength
Let his bed be covered with earth's black flint strength
Let the lightning cross over his head.

As this prayer makes clear, another area of deep concern was the cultivation of a spiritual understanding of the world. So crucial was the power earned in visions and dreams that those who failed to attain it were left to feel second-best, as shown by the contrasting life stories of Sam Newland and Jack Stewart, published by Julian H. Steward as *Two Paiute Autobiographies*. Jack Stewart had a series of dreams that made him a successful hunter, and then a defining vision in which Birch Mountain—one of the highest of the Sierra Nevada peaks—offered him power and protection. But Sam Newland was a failure at the hunt and, he tells us sadly, "I never did dream of a power."

So among the accounts of the true and deep childhood visions that sustained men such as Black Elk for a lifetime, I also include in this book the story of Sam Blowsnake's vision quest—how he waited, fasting and crying to the spirits for four nights without experiencing anything other than cold, hunger, and fear, and how in the end he lied, telling everyone that he had been blessed by the spirits. "I was not telling the truth, yet they gave me the food that is carefully prepared for those who have been blessed."

I have tried in this mesh of childhood memories to include contrasting episodes such as these, the warp and the weave of the expected pattern, in the hope that the result will be true not only to the Native American idea of childhood as a life lived in and for the community but also to the unique experience of the individuals whose words make up this braid of lives.

NEIL PHILIP

Carl Moon *Tale of the Tribe* c. 1910

# THE WORLD AROUND US

There were always kids around my grandpa, and he was always teaching us, getting us to watch, to listen to nature and the world around us. Grandpa would take us out into the Badlands and show us fossils and the layers of rock. He would tell us about the many ages when these rocks had been laid down, when these ancient animals had lived. He told us that the rocks had seen many things through the centuries while they watched the stars and the sun and the moon. The rocks had many things to teach us about the ancient history of the Earth Mother.

Grandpa taught us about the ways and habits of the animals. He would say, "We were the last to be created. The animals are our elder relations and have much wisdom to teach. They walk the way of the earth and the ways they were given by the Creator. Whoever walks the way of the earth walks a good road."

And Grandpa always taught us to walk carefully, to be aware of every little thing. One day we were walking along by the creek that ran behind my grandpa's place. There was an old, brown, dried-up log in the path that I always had to climb over.

"How many times have you climbed right over this log?" Grandpa asked. "Let me show you something. There is a whole world right here."

Grandpa lifted up the log and told me to get down and look closely. I got down on my knees and peered under the log. Grandpa was right: there was a whole world under there. Bugs were running around in all directions. Some of them were scurrying around gathering up food. Others seemed to be trying to save their little home.

Grandpa put the log back carefully and told me, "Just as we are looking at their world, there is someone who is looking down on us. This is their little world. They go out from their village to hunt and

1

gather food, and they bring it home to their people. We have no reason to disturb their world. Someone could come along and take this log, and maybe if they're careful and don't disturb things too much, these bugs can find another log or someplace to live. If you were starving, you might have to eat some of them, but there's no reason to destroy the whole village.

"Whenever we see living things, we must respect their right to live. They are our relatives. We disturb them or eat them only when we have to, to survive. Whenever we do that, we leave a space, a hole in the Creator's world. Go to your uncles and see what they do. When they kill a deer, they put tobacco there and talk to their brother. When they release the spirit, they put down tobacco to help in a humble way to cover that hole they made in the world. They ask the Creator to accept their small offering and prayer, for it is the best we can do as pitiful human beings."

Louis Two Ravens Irwin
MANDAN /HIDATSA/ARIKARA

1933–1995, speaking c. 1990

Edward S. Curtis *Offering the buffalo skull* Mandan 1908

# CRYING TO THE SPIRITS

Father and Mother had four children, and after that I was born, it is said. An uncle of Mother's who was named White-Cloud said to her, "You are to give birth to a child who will not be an ordinary person." Thus he spoke to her. It was then my mother gave birth to me. As soon as I was born and was being washed—as my neck was being washed—I laughed out loudly.

   I was a good-tempered boy, it is said. At boyhood my father told me to fast and I obeyed. In the winter every morning I would crush charcoal and blacken my face with it. I would arise very early and do it. As soon as the sun rose, I would go outside and sit looking at the sun, and I would cry to the spirits.

**Sam Blowsnake**   *Big Winnebago*
WINNEBAGO   *Hotcangara*

born c. 1875, writing c. 1917

# THE GREAT SPIRIT

I was out early and late in quest of the favors of the manitous [spirits], who, it was said, were numerous—who filled the air! At early dawn I watched the rising of the palace of the Great Spirit—the sun—who, it was said, made the world!

Early as I can recollect, I was taught that it was the gift of the many spirits to be a good hunter and warrior; and much of my time I devoted in search of their favors. On the mountain top, or along the valley or the water brook, I searched for some kind intimation from the spirits who made their residence in the noise of the waterfalls.

I dreaded to hear the voice of the angry spirit in the gathering clouds. I looked with anxiety to catch a glimpse of the wings of the Great Spirit, who shrouded himself in rolling white and dark clouds—who, with his wings, fanned the earth, and laid low the tall pines and hemlock in his course—who rode in whirlwinds and tornadoes, and plucked the trees from their woven roots—who chased other gods from his course—who drove the bad spirit from the surface of the earth, down to the dark caverns of the deep.

Yet he was a kind spirit. My father taught me to call that spirit Gichi-manitou—Benevolent spirit—for his ancestors taught him no other name to give to that spirit who made the earth, with all its variety and smiling beauty.

His benevolence I saw in the running of the streams, for the animals to quench their thirst and the fishes to live; the fruit of the earth teemed wherever I looked. Everything I saw smilingly said, *Gichi-manitou nin-ge-oo-she-ig*—The benevolent spirit made me.

George Copway   *Kah-ge-ga-gah-bowh*
CHIPPEWA  *Ojibwa*

born 1818, writing in 1850

# HOW I GOT MY NAME

When I was born, my grandmother had built a hut some distance away. Then my mother went off into this hut. There I was born. So there my mother remained. My grandmother would go there to make fire and to cook her daughter's meals.

On the third day was when I began to cry, calling for shinney-bags and for a red blouse and for red and blue silk ribbons. But I was not given these things. Then my mother got well. She called in an old woman who was supposed to understand the speech of infants. So that old woman came.

"What ails you that you cry all the time? You are tormenting your mother."

"Why, they do not give me my shinney-bags and my blouse and my ribbons. That is why I cry. If my mother does not give me them, I shall go back whence I came."

"Very well; cease crying, little one. You mother will give you shinney-bags and a blouse and ribbons. But cease crying."

Then my mother gave me all these things, and I stopped crying.

After a while again I became very sick and again cried all the time. Then again the old woman was called in to come and ask me why I wept.

"Why, my name is not Kusiahkiw: otherwise am I called."

"Then what are you called, little one?"

"Maskwawanahkwatok (Red Cloud Woman) I am called."

"Then so shall you be called. Do not ever weep again."

That is all.

Louise Dutchman    *Maskwawanahkwatok*
MENOMINI

born c. 1870, speaking c. 1920

Edward S. Curtis *Assiniboin mother and child* 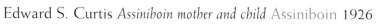 Assiniboin 1926

# I TRIED TO BE LIKE MY MOTHER

I tried to be like my mother. . . . I carried my doll on my back just as mothers carry their babies; and besides this I had a little tipi that I pitched whenever my aunt pitched hers. It was made exactly like my aunt's, had the same number of poles—only, of course, my tipi was very small. My horse dragged the poles and packed the lodge-skin, so that I often beat my aunt in setting up my lodge, which she pretended made her jealous. And how I used to hurry in setting up my lodge, so that I might have a fire going inside it before my aunt could kindle one in hers! I did not know it then, but now I feel sure that she often let me beat her just to encourage me.

Each year, as was our custom, I made myself a new lodge and set it up, as the grownups did, when we went into our winter camps. Each time I made a new one I cut my lodge-skin larger than the old one, took more and more pains to have it pretty. I played with these little lodges, often lived in them, until I was a married woman, and even after. I have never lost my love for play.

Once several of us girls made ourselves a play village with our tiny tipis. Of course, our children were dolls, and our horses dogs, and yet we managed to make our village look very real, so real that we thought we ought to have some meat to cook. We decided to kill it ourselves. A girl named Beaver-that-passes and I said we would be the hunters, that we would go out to a buffalo herd that was in sight and kill a calf. Knowing that we could not handle a bow, Beaver-that-passes borrowed her father's lance that was very sharp, and longer than both our bodies put together. We caught and saddled two gentle pack-horses; and both the old fools went crazy before we managed to kill a calf. I helped all I could, but it was Beaver-that-passes who wounded a big calf that gave us both a lot of trouble before we

Edward S. Curtis *A child's lodge* Piegan 1910

finally got it down, and dead. I hurt my leg, and Beaver-that-passes cut her hand with the lance. The calf itself looked pretty bad by the time we got it to our play village. But we had a big feast and forgot our hurts.

And that night we had great fun. The moon was big, as big as it ever gets, and very white. The lodges in the big village made pretty shadows, and everywhere people were laughing. The night was just chilly enough so that fires were burning in all the lodges. To make them smoke and bother the old people, we girls stole about the village pulling the poles out of the smoke-ears of the lodges, letting them fall down. This was sure to bring some woman out to scold the moon-shadows, because she could not see us. One old woman pretended that she saw us, running straight at us with her root-digger in her hand. *Tst, tst, tst!* The things she said! But we stood still, knowing that she could not see us unless we moved. I was glad when that old woman fixed her smoke-ears and went back into her lodge. It is difficult to stand still that way when you are not exactly sure of yourself.


Pretty-shield
CROW *Absaroke*

born c. 1857, speaking c. 1930

Irwin and Mankins *Kiowa girl* Kiowa 1890s

# WHEN WE WERE QUITE SMALL BOYS

When we were quite small boys, we would go out hunting horses, and bring back a dog and call it a horse. When we made a new camp, we seldom stayed more than ten days. In that way our health was sustained by travel. While we were on the move from one camp to another, we had to cross wide streams. We boys would measure the width of the river and compete with each other to see who could swim across without stopping. I am telling you now what I did to build myself up to be the man I am now. The boys who were the same age and size as myself would wrestle, and if a boy downed me three or four times, I kept up the practice of wrestling until I had more strength. Then I could throw this boy, and I was satisfied. I selected a boy to run a race; if the boy passed me, then I made the distance longer, and if he passed me again, I made the distance still longer, for I knew that I was long-winded. Then I won the race.

Fifteen or twenty of us boys would go out to the river and daub ourselves up with mud and so disguise ourselves that no one in the camp would know us Then we would take jerked buffalo beef that the women had hung up around the camp to dry and go off out of sight and have a feast. None of us was caught at it, because they could not tell one boy from another.

**White Man Runs Him**   *Mias-tas-hede-karoos*
CROW   *Absaroke*

born 1844, speaking in 1909

Edward S. Curtis *White Man Runs Him* Crow 1908

# THE OLD MAN

When a child is mischievous, they call an old man who looks fierce. He is no relative. The old man limps in with a sack or blanket in his hand. He acts angry and shouts, "What's the matter?"

The father and the mother sit there. They say, "This boy won't obey. He is always fighting. You can take him and do what you wish with him. You can cut off his head or sit on him. We don't care. We aren't going to put up with him any longer." The boy begins to cry.

The old man says, "So, you won't obey? I'm going to check you off right now." The boy cries louder.

"Now stop that! Listen to me. Come over to me or I'm going to get you." The child is frightened. He tries to crawl behind his father, his mother, or his grandmother. But they act as if they have given the old man the privilege to do what he wants with the boy, and they push the boy forward. Then the old man grabs him and struggles with him. He puts him in the sack and says, "Are you going to behave?"

After that the boy is prompt and behaves. If he won't get wood, his mother says, "All right, I'll call the old man." Then the boy goes for the wood at once. After the old man works on him like this two or three times, he comes to be a good boy.

These old men look fierce and funny. The children are afraid of them. The old man is never the grandparent. It is always an outsider. The grandparent is there with the parents to see the child get his lesson.

Anonymous man
CHIRICAHUA APACHE   *Inde*

speaking in the 1930s

Gerhard sisters *Geronimo* Apache 1904

14

# WE WERE VERY POOR

I and my brother were both small, and we lived alone with our grandmother at her peach orchard. We were very poor. There was no meat. Our grandmother made corn cakes for us, and these we ate. When the corn was ripe, grandmother made us fresh cornbread and *hepaloka*, fresh corn *hepaloka*. We were very poor. We stayed with her alone at our peach orchard. Every day we ate *hampasa* [a yellow flowered herb], dipping it in water. We were living alone with our grandmother and our grandfather. We were very poor.

Our grandmother said, "Children, go to your mother and your father at Caliente. There your mother is staying, your father is staying. I think they have meat, your mother and father. Now, you go ahead." Grandfather saddled a burro for us. We were going to Caliente, I and my brother. We were very poor. We wanted a little piece of meat. At the peach orchard, brother mounted his burro. Grandfather took me in his arms and lifted me on to my burro. There was one burro. My brother mounted. My grandfather lifted me up on the burro where my brother was mounted. We went.

At Caliente my mother and my father were staying alone. My father killed deer. Many deer he killed. "Hiya! My two children are coming. Why have you come?" "Our grandmother wants meat very badly, therefore we have come." "Hurry up," he said. "The two children want meat at their peach orchard."

My mother wrapped up lots of meat for me. We mounted our burro. When we were small, we were very poor with our grandfather and our grandmother. We were living alone at the peach orchard. We were lonely, we cried.


Lina Zuñi
ZUÑI   *A'shiwi*

born c. 1856, speaking in 1926


Edward S. Curtis *The melon eaters* Hopi 1900

# MY GRANDFATHER

When I was a pretty small boy, my grandmother used to tell me, "Always wear your moccasins when you walk around. Don't run around with your hair blowing everywhere." She braided my hair for me. My mother told her to raise me right and take care of me.

I had two dogs that I played with. My grandfather fixed a rope for me to lasso the dogs with and lead them around by. He made me a set of arrows and a bow. The arrows were blunt-ended and the bow was small, like children used. He told me not to shoot at anything except birds. He told me, "Certain boys go way off when they play. Don't go with them because they are crazy." He said to swim only with boys my own size, because big boys might drown me. I would play around with my bow and arrow until I got tired of it; then I would rope my dogs and pretend they were horses. When my father went out to round up his horses, I rode with him, on the back of the saddle. He showed me how to stop a horse to catch it. I would hold out my hand like I was going to feed him and then he would stop. I learned how to hobble horses, too.

My grandfather used to get me up early. Before that I sometimes slept late. He would say, "Get up! Wash your face and comb your hair."

One time he caught one of his gentlest horses and told me, "Ride him bareback." In the evening I rode that horse as we took the other horses to be watered. That is how he taught me to ride. When I had learned, he pointed out a certain boy who liked to hunt. He told me, "Go with him to chase rabbits and shoot birds." Sometimes we brought in rabbits to eat.

One morning my grandfather got me up early and said, "Take your horse. Put the bridle on him and go out and water our horses. Take off the hobbles and put the ropes around their necks. Take them down to the water. You have seen how I do it." I did it myself that time.

As I went around with other boys chasing rabbits and squirrels, some of us got to be pretty good shots with a bow and arrow. Later I was taught to shoot a .44 Winchester. My grandfather took me out by a hill and put down a bone for a target. He showed me how to sight with the rifle. At first I was a little afraid. I didn't shoot very well at the beginning; the bullets just went off anywhere. My grandfather never let me have the rifle; he always kept it. He explained to me how to sight with the rifle. By this time I was growing up to be a pretty good-sized boy.

Then my grandfather gave me a rope, a bridle, and saddle. He said I knew how to handle horses and could go about it myself. The saddle had a case on it for the rifle. Then he gave me the rifle.

Sometime before the country opened up, my grandfather died. They didn't kill his horse at the funeral or anything like that in the old-time way. My father said to me, "Now that your grandfather is gone, some of these horses will be yours. Take care of them as he taught you to." My grandfather, before he died, had told my father which of the horses were to be mine.

Jim Whitewolf
KIOWA APACHE   *Nadíisha-déna*

born c. 1878, speaking c. 1948

# THIS IS YOUR CAMP

As far back as I can remember, my father and mother directed me how to act. They used to tell me, "Do not use a bad word which you wouldn't like to be used to you. Do not feel that you are anyone's enemy. In playing with children, remember this: do not take anything from another child. Don't take arrows away from another boy just because you are bigger than he is. Don't take his marbles away. Don't steal from your own friends. Don't be unkind to your playmates. If you are kind now, when you become a man you will love your fellow men.

"When you go to the creek and swim, don't duck anyone's children. Don't ever fight a girl when you're playing with other children. Girls are weaker than boys. If you fight with them, that will cause us trouble with our neighbors.

"Don't laugh at feeble old men and women. That's the worst thing you can do. Don't criticize them and make fun of them. Don't laugh at anybody or make fun of anybody.

"This is your camp. What little we have here is for you to eat. Don't go to another camp with other children for a meal. Come back to your own camp when you are hungry and then go out and play again.

"When you start to eat, act like a grown person. Just wait until things are served to you. Do not take bread or a drink or a piece of meat before the rest start to eat. Don't ask before the meal for things that are still cooking, as many children do. Don't try to eat more than you want. Try to be just as polite as you can; sit still while you eat. Do not step over another person, going around and reaching for something.

"Don't run into another person's camp as though it was your own. Don't run around anyone's camp. When you go to another camp, don't stand at the door. Go right in and sit down like a grown person.

Don't get into their drinking water. Don't go out and catch or hobble horses and ride them as if they belonged to you the way some boys do. Do not throw stones at anybody's animals.

"When a visitor comes, do not go in front of him or step over him. Do not cut up while the visitor is here. If you want to play, get up quietly, go behind the visitor and out the door."

Anonymous man
CHIRICAHUA APACHE  *Inde*

speaking in the 1930s

Edward S. Curtis *Apache camp* Apache 1906

21

# MARCHING AROUND

The first thing our older playfellows taught us to do was to go around to the different houses in the evening. We marched around, and this is the name of the game—"Marching Around." We go in a string, one boy after another. There used to be a lot of us. There must have been fifty boys in Fort Rupert at that time. We bent our backs and put our thumbs in our mouths, stretching our lips wide, stamping our feet, and singing, "Bend down, place of names." Then any of the household that has a feeling tells the boys to sit down by the fire, and they give us something to eat—sometimes the fat of the mountain goat, sometimes dried berries, anything the boys like. We eat, and then go to another house. If we are lucky, they all give us something to eat, and when we are full, we stop.

Another game like this we used to do at nighttime, close to bedtime. We used to go from house to house, feel what is in their house that we would like to eat. We call the name of a noble child, usually a girl, that is in the house. We say all this and knock on the outside of the house, calling out, "Turn over to your little box and get out the grub from your box." They will say, "Come in and sit down." They will get some kind of food and give it to us. Then we will go to another house. If one house don't call us in, we take sticks and beat them on the house, singing, "We don't think you are loved by anyone." When we get full, we go home and go to bed.

**Charles James Nowell** *Tlalis* (Stranded Whale)
KWAKIUTL

born 1870, speaking in 1940

22

ABOVE: Elbridge Warren Merrill *The Sitka Village* Tlingit c. 1904

FOLLOWING PAGE: H. T. Cory *Angelic LaMoose* Flathead 1913

23

# DOLLS NEVER APPEALED TO ME

My mother and grandmother made dolls of buckskin stuffed with deer hair, with red seeds for eyes and wisps of horse tail glued on the head for hair, but dolls never appealed to me. I preferred playing with the bows and arrows my father made for me or listening to old men tell stories of warfare and horrible bloodshed. Most of all, I loved my dogs. The village was full of them. They were very ordinary— mongrels, really—but to me they were wonderful, faithful creatures who would follow me everywhere on my play hunts for deer and along imaginary war trails.

For more excitement, we played with calves and horses. Boys would chase a calf that was wild and had never been tied before. They would try to ride it, but the back was often wet from sweat, and there was no mane to hold on to. Sometimes they would try to ride a colt. If it became tired and panting, then I could often stay on its back for a short period. When the boys were weary of the animals, they showed off . . . . They would jump over rails to show off their physical agility. I stood in admiration until the boys began to tease me to join them. I tried to jump the rail but missed and was thrown to the ground, bruising my shins. I choked back tears, afraid my cousins would call me an old woman or a crybaby. For many days afterward, however, I practiced until I could briefly ride the colt and calf or beat boys at the footrace and broad jump. The animals grew accustomed to me, and my muscles were hard and strong by the time I had my own pony.

**Mourning Dove**   (Christine Quintasket)
SALISHAN   *Swhy-ayl-puh*

c. 1885–1936, writing in the 1930s

25

# WE PLAYED AT GETTING MARRIED

We children used to build play wickiups. Some of them were as high as one arm span. We built little fires inside them, just like a real wickiup. We played at getting married and having families. Girls and boys played together at this. When we played at marriage, we were always careful not to marry some child who was of our own clan, just as big people were. We played at marriage negotiations, the girl's family and boy's family exchanging large gifts of food. The food was made of mud and water. When it came time for the presentation of these gifts, the members of the family receiving them would all line up on one side to get their share. Sometimes we would make a gift of horses to the other family. The horses were boys.

Anna Price

EASTERN WHITE MOUNTAIN APACHE  *Inde*

c. 1837–1937, speaking c. 1930

# MORNING-STANDS-UP

We lived at Mesquite Root, and my father was chief there. That was a good place, high up among the hills, but flat, with a little wash where you could plant corn. Prickly pear grew there so thick that in summer, when you picked the fruit, it was only four steps from one bush to the next. And cholla cactus grew, and there were ironwood trees. Good nuts they have! There were birds flying around—doves and woodpeckers—and a big rabbit sometimes in the early morning, and quails running across the flat land. Right above us was Quijotoa Mountain, the one where the cloud stands up high and white when we sing for rain.

We lived in a grass house, and our relatives, all around us on the smooth flat land, had houses that were the same. Round our houses were, with no smoke hole and just a little door where you crawled in on hands and knees. That was good. The smoke could go out anywhere through the thatch and the air could come in. All our family slept on cactus fiber mats against the wall, pushed tight against it so centipedes and scorpions could not crawl in.

William Dinwiddie *Papago woman in front of her home* Papago c. 1894

There was a mat for each two children, but no, nothing over us. When we were cold, we put wood on the fire.

Early in the morning, in the month of Pleasant Cold, when we had all slept in the house to keep warm, we would wake in the dark to hear my father speaking.

"Open your ears, for I am telling you a good thing. Wake up and listen. Open your ears. Let my words enter them." He spoke in a low voice, so quiet in the dark. Always our fathers spoke to us like that, so low that you thought you were dreaming.

"Wake up and listen. You boys, you should go out and run. So you will be swift in time of war. You girls, you should grind the corn. So you will feed the men, and they will fight the enemy. You should practice running. So in time of war you may save your lives."

For a long time my father talked to us like that, for he began when it was black dark. I went to sleep, and then he pinched my ear. "Wake up! Do not be idle!"

Then we got up. It was the time we call morning-stands-up, when it is dark, but there are white lines in the east. Those are the white hairs of Elder Brother who made us. He put them there so we can know when day is coming and we can go out to look for food.

We crawled out the little door. I remember that door so well. I always crawled out of doors till long after I was a married woman and we stopped being afraid of enemies. Then we made houses with white men's doors. But this one was little, and when we came out, we could see the houses of my relatives nearby among the cactus, and the girls coming out of them, too, to get water.


Maria Chona
PAPAGO   *Tohono O'odham*

born c. 1846, speaking c. 1932

# LEARNING TO RUN

The day was in summer, the world green and very beautiful. I was playing with some other boys when my grandfather stopped to watch. "Take off your shirt and leggings," he said to me.

I tore them from my back and legs, and, naked except for my moccasins, stood before him.

"Now catch me that yellow butterfly," he ordered. "Be quick!"

Away I went after the yellow butterfly. How fast these creatures are, and how cunning! In and out among the trees and bushes, across streams, over grassy places, now low near the ground, then just above my head, the dodging butterfly led me far before I caught and held it in my hand. Panting, but concealing my shortness of breath as best I could, I offered it to Grandfather, who whispered, as though he told me a secret: "Rub its wings over your heart, my son, and ask the butterflies to lend you their grace and swiftness."

Plenty-coups  *Aleek-chea-ahoosh*
CROW  *Absároke*

1847–1932, speaking in 1928

FOLLOWING PAGE:
John Alvin Anderson *Ben Reifel playing a love flute* Sioux c. 1925

# AN INDIAN MUST ALWAYS RISE EARLY

Indian children were trained so that they hardly ever cried much in the night. This was very expedient and necessary in their exposed life. In my infancy it was my grandmother's custom to put me to sleep, as she said, with the birds, and to waken me with them, until it became a habit. She did this with an object in view. An Indian must always rise early. In the first place, as a hunter, he finds his game best at daybreak. Secondly, other tribes, when on the warpath, usually make their attack very early in the morning. Even when our people are moving about leisurely, we like to rise before daybreak, in order to travel when the air is cool, and unobserved, perchance, by our enemies.

As a little child, it was instilled into me to be silent and reticent. This was one of the most important traits to form in the character of the Indian. As a hunter and warrior it was considered absolutely necessary to him, and was thought to lay the foundations of patience and self-control. There are times when boisterous mirth is indulged in by our people, but the rule is gravity and decorum.

After all, my babyhood was full of interest and the beginnings of life's realities. The spirit of daring was already whispered into my ears. The value of the eagle feather as worn by the warrior had caught my eye. One day, when I was left alone, at scarcely two years of age, I took my uncle's war bonnet and plucked out all its eagle feathers to decorate my dog and myself. So soon the life that was about me had made its impress, and already I desired intensely to comply with all of its demands.

Charles A. Eastman    *Ohiyesa*
WAHPETON SIOUX    *Dakota*

1858–1939, writing c. 1900

# RACING UNDER THE SUN

About this time I used to race by myself early in the morning while it was still dark, and in the middle of the day, and in the evening. In the middle of the day when it got real hot, when the sun was right in the middle of the sky, I used to run a race under the sun, while the sun was looking down on me. That's the time the sun is having dinner. When he sees me running a race under him, he'll try to get me a horse. The sun that we see in the sky is our father, and I'm his son; that's why when I race under him, when he sees me running, he knows I'm after something, he knows I'm after a horse. And soon enough I'll get a horse from my father, the sun, and from there on I won't be on foot anymore. It's as when you're working for something, trying your best to get it. Even though it's hard to get, you must try and try to get the thing you want. That's the way I used to be; I worked hard for everything.

In the summertime I used to put a lot of sand in my moccasins. I'd squeeze my feet into them even though it hurt. At first I had a hard time running, but after a while I began to get used to it. From there on I hardly knew I had dirt in my moccasins; it seemed to me as though I had nothing in them; I could carry it all as far as I wanted to go. I put the sand in my moccasins to toughen my feet, so as to be able to run anywhere, through sand and through snow and not mind it, so that when I wanted to go through the sand and the desert I could stand it, even though the sand was deep, without getting tired, even though the snow was twelve inches deep or more I could run through it as though there were nothing on the ground.

Edward S. Curtis *A son of the desert* Navajo 1904

That's how I raced for six miles in order to make my feet and legs strong and my muscles hard. And I used to take a mouthful of water and, holding it in my mouth, run up a great big hill. I did this so as to develop strong wind. I breathed only through my nose while running.

In the winter, when the snow was on the ground, not the first snow that comes but the second—the second, you know, is colder than the first—I used to race early in the morning while it was still dark. Even though it was a real cold morning, I had to get up without anything on, except my moccasins and G-string, and run for a long distance. While I'd be running on my way, I'd go under a young tree and shake the snow on myself. This was a hard thing to do. If you're not strong, every time you shake the snow onto yourself, you'll say, *Ah!* Before I'd start back for home I'd throw myself in the snow and roll around in it for quite a while. When I'd get home, I wouldn't go inside. I'd stop by the doorway, turn around again, and run for the water. If there was thick ice on top of the water, I'd get a stick or a piece of rock, break the ice, take off my moccasins, and jump in. I'd stay in the icy water as long as I could stand it, turning over and over hollering and screaming so as to develop a good voice. Then I'd get out and put on my moccasins and start for home. While I'd be running on my way, my body would be covered with a thin coat of ice, cracking all over me.

Left Handed
NAVAJO  *Diné*

born 1868, speaking in 1934

# AH, HOW WE COULD RUN

Ah, how we could run, we Desert People; all the morning until the sun was high, without once stopping! My brothers took their bows and arrows and went far off over the flat land.

"Run," my father said to them. "Run until you are exhausted. So you will be a strong man. If you fall down tired, far out in the wasteland, perhaps a vision will come to you. Perhaps a hawk will visit you and teach you to be swift. Perhaps you will get a piece of the rainbow to carry on your shoulder so that no one can get near to you, anymore than to the rainbow itself. Or maybe Coyote himself will sing you a song that has magic in it."

So they went off in their breechcloths and bare feet, running in the dark when they could hardly see the cactus joints on the ground and the horned toads—rattlesnakes there were not in that cool weather. One of my brothers did really have visions. The others used to come back without him, bringing jackrabbits for our dinner. The little boy would come in much later and never tell where he had been. But we found out long, long after, when he became a medicine man, that he had been lying dead out on the desert all those hours and that Coyote had come and talked to him.

Maria Chona
PAPAGO   *Tohono O'odham*

born c. 1846, speaking c. 1932

# EARLY MORNING SWIMS

I think I must have been about eight years old when I first started to swim and run in the early morning. That may be what has kept me from growing tall. I never refused to do anything my parents asked of me. They told me to do these things. I saw other children doing them, so I did them, too. That's the way we made our hearts strong. I used to swim with other children, and several of them were girls of my own age.

John Rope
WESTERN WHITE MOUNTAIN APACHE    *Inde*


When I was about nine or ten, the daughter of my mother's blood sister came and took me from my maternal uncle, who up until that time had cared for me. She thought I was not being raised the way a girl should. She was a grown and married woman, and I called her my older sister. She started in to train me. I could not sleep well, for she made me get up early in the morning and run and bathe in the river. She used to drag me right out of the wickiup sometimes to make me do it. In wintertime when I swam in the river, the current would sweep me against the ice and my body would be scraped. I thought it was awful at the time, but now I can appreciate that it was the right thing for me.

Mrs. Andrew Stanley
EASTERN WHITE MOUNTAIN APACHE    *Inde*

both speaking c. 1930

Edward S. Curtis *The morning bath* Apache 1906

# WE HAD LOTS OF GAMES

We had lots of games. Some of them were pretty simple, but they were great sport for us and I guess you could say they kept us out of mischief. One game was pretty much like shinny. The ball was made out of buckskin stuffed with deer hair, and the players all had specially shaped sticks to knock it around with. Hopis call that game *nahoydadatsia*, Tewas call it *buntamaylay*. There was a sloping piece of clear ground, and we used to play over there. This game is the one the two warrior gods, Pokanghoya and Palengahoya, are supposed to be playing all the time. You hear about it in the old stories.

We also had a dart-throwing game. We made the darts out of corncobs, with feathers at one end and a sharp greasewood point at the other. We had teams. We would throw at a target made out of corn leaves, or something like that, or throw at hoops. Another game we had that was great fun for the boys was a sort of throwing race with corncobs. You'd have a corncob, or a ball as a substitute, tied to a string, and the other end of the string was tied to a little crosspiece made of wood. A boy would put the crosspiece between his toes, lie down on his back, and flip the corncob with his foot as far as he could over his head. Then another boy would flip it. The last boy down the line would start the corncob going back the other way. Whichever side got its corncob back to the starting place was the winner. We also had another corncob game, but we played it a little differently. The objective was to throw the corncob down into the kiva.

Albert Yava   *Big Falling Snow*
Tewa/Hopi

born 1888, speaking c. 1969

Frederick Monsen *The sentinels* Hopi 1908

# THINGS I WAS TOLD NOT TO DO

Things I was told not to do—I did them. I liked to play rough. We played shinny ball, a kind of hockey game. We made the ball and sticks ourselves. We played the hoop game, shot with a bow and arrow. We had foot races, horse races, and water races. We liked to play *mato kiciyapi*, the bear game, throwing sharp, stiff grass stems at each other. These could really hurt you and draw blood if they hit the bare skin. And we were always at the *isto kicicastakapi*, the pit-slinging game. You chewed the fruit from the rosebush or wild cherries, spat a fistful of pits into your hand, and flung them into the other fellow's face. And of course I liked the Grab-Them-by-the-Hair-and-Kick-Them game, which we played with two teams.

I liked to ride horseback behind my older sister, holding on to her. As I got a little bigger, she would hold on to me. By the time I was nine years old I had my own horse to ride. It was a beautiful gray pony my father had given me together with a fine saddle and a very colorful Mexican saddle blanket. That gray was my favorite companion, and I was proud to ride him. But he was not mine for long. I lost him through my own fault.

*Nonge Pahloka*—the Piercing of Her Ears—is a big event in a little girl's life. By this ceremony her parents, and especially her grandmother, want to show how much they love and honor her. They ask a man who is respected for his bravery or wisdom to pierce the ears of their daughter. The grandmother puts on a big feed. The little girl is placed on a blanket surrounded by the many gifts her family will give away in her name. The man who does the piercing is much admired and gets the most valuable gift. Afterward they get down to the really important part—the eating.

Well, one day I watched somebody pierce a girl's ears. I saw the fuss they made over it, the presents he got and all that. I thought I should do this to my little sister. She was about four years old at the time and I was nine. I don't know anymore what made me want to do this. Maybe I wanted to feel big and important like the man whom I had watched perform the ceremony. Maybe I wanted to get a big present. Maybe I wanted to make my sister cry. I don't remember what was in my little boy's mind then. I found some wire and made a pair of "ear rings" out of it. Then I asked my sister, "Would you like me to put these on you?" She smiled. "*Ohan*—yes." I didn't have the sharp bone one uses for the ear-piercing, and I didn't know the prayer that goes with it. I just had an old awl but thought this would do fine. Oh, how my sister yelled. I had to hold her down, but I got that awl through her earlobes and managed to put the "ear rings" in. I was proud of the neat job I had done.

When my mother came home and saw those wire loops in my sister's ears, she gasped. But she recovered soon enough to go and tell my father. That was one of the few occasions he talked to me. He said, "I should punish you and whip you, but I won't. That's not my way. You'll get your punishment later." Well, some time passed and I forgot all about it. One morning my father announced that we were going to a powwow. He had hitched up the wagon and it was heaped high with boxes and bundles. At that powwow my father let it be known that he was doing a big *otuhan*—a giveaway. He put my sister on a rug, a pretty Navajo blanket, and laid out things to give away—quilts, food, blankets, a fine shotgun, his own new pair of cowboy boots, a sheepskin coat—enough to fit out a whole family. Dad was telling the people, "I want to honor my daughter for her ear-piercing. This should have been done openly, but my son did it at home. I guess he's too small. He didn't know any better." This was a long speech for Dad. He motioned me to come closer. I was sitting on my pretty gray horse. I thought we were both cutting a very fine figure. Well, before I knew it, Dad had given my horse away, together with its beautiful saddle and blanket. I had to ride home in the wagon and cried all the way. The old man said, "You have your punishment now, but you will feel better later on. All her life your sister will tell about how you pierced her ears. She'll brag about you.

I bet you are the only small boy who ever did this big ceremony."

 That was no consolation to me. My beautiful gray was gone. I was heartbroken for three days. On the fourth morning I looked out the door and there stood a little white stallion with a new saddle and a silver-plated bit. "It's yours," my father told me. "Get on it." I was happy again.

**Lame Deer** (John Fire)  *Tahce Ushte*
MINICONJOU SIOUX  *Lakota*

born c. 1900, speaking c. 1966

Jesse Hastings Bratley *Harry with Horns* Sioux 1890s

# I WAS A WILD LITTLE GIRL

I was a wild little girl of seven. Loosely clad in a slip of brown buckskin, and lightfooted with a pair of soft moccasins on my feet, I was as free as the wind that blew my hair, and no less spirited than a bounding deer. These were my mother's pride—my wild freedom and overflowing spirits. She taught me no fear, save that of intruding myself upon others.

Having gone many paces ahead, I stopped, panting for breath and laughing with glee as my mother watched my every movement. I was not wholly conscious of myself, but was more keenly alive to the fire within. It was as if I were the activity, and my hands and feet were only experiments for my spirit to work upon.

**Gertrude Bonnin** *Zitkala-Ṡa*
YANKTON SIOUX *Nakota*

1878–1938, writing in 1899

Richard Throssel *A Cheyenne warrior of the future* Cheyenne 1907

# PLAYING WAR

When it was summer again, we were camping on the Rosebud, and I did not feel so much afraid, because the Wasichus [white people] seemed farther away and there was peace there in the valley and there was plenty of meat. But all the boys from five or six years up were playing war. The little boys would gather together from the different bands of the tribe and fight each other with mud balls that they threw with willow sticks. And the big boys played the game called Throwing-Them-off-Their-Horses, which is a battle—all but the killing—and sometimes they got hurt. The horsebacks from the different bands would line up and charge upon each other, yelling. And when the ponies came together on the run, they would rear and flounder and scream in a big dust, and the riders would seize each other, wrestling until one side had lost all its men, for those who fell upon the ground were counted dead.

When I was older, I, too, often played this game. We were always naked when we played it, just as warriors are when they go into battle if it is not too cold, because they are swifter without clothes. Once I fell off on my back right in the middle of a bed of prickly pears, and it took my mother a long while to pick all the stickers out of me. I was still too little to play war that summer, but I can remember watching the other boys, and I thought that when we all grew up and were big together, maybe we could kill all the Wasichus or drive them far away from our country.


**Black Elk**  *Hehaka Sapa*
OGLALA SIOUX  *Lakota*

1863–1950, speaking in 1931

# SOME OF THE KIDS WOULD TEASE ME

We used to play a game like baseball, where we would throw a ball at the front of the big house. One fella would hit the ball and bounce it against the house and then run while we would try to hit him. We would go down to the beach every day and play with little boats. We made little boats and dragged them in the water along the beach. All the kids in the village would be down there playing with their little boats, and sometimes we would take a dugout canoe and row around in front of the island.

Some of the kids would tease me about not having a father. They would say, "You got no father, your father died," and all that. I used to feel awfully bad. I would go right home and stay away from those fellas. I never used to fight back, because my mother and my grandparents used to say to me that if any of those kids wanted to fight I shouldn't ever fight with them. I was told to just stay away from them. I always did that and never fought back, because they were very strict with the potlatch rule at that time. They told me, "If you fight with the other kids, then it is going to cost us money and we will have to give a potlatch." I remember that some of the other kids who were related to me got into quarrels with some of the others. They called all the people together right away and announced it in public what they had done and then they gave some stuff away. I remember that they gave away flour, boxes of biscuits, and a pile of biscuit dough in boxes.

In the evenings we were not allowed to go out. We had to stay home, and they used to tell me that if I went out and walked along in the village the ghosts would grab me and twist me around and twist my face. I used to be scared.

Anon. *James Sewid held by his grandmother Lucy Sewid, Alert Bay* Kwakiutl c. 1914

At night they would build a big fire in the middle of the house, and when it was time to go to sleep we would all sit around the fire and some of the older people would be telling the stories. It was a big open fire, and we were all little kids sitting around it. I remember best the stories about Tlislagila, which means Little Mink, child of the sun. They called the sun Tlisla.

James Sewid
KWAKIUTL  *Kwiksutainuk/Mamalilikulla*

born 1913, speaking c. 1967

47

John K. Hillers *Hopi rabbit hunters* Hopi 1879

# LEARNING TO WORK

Learning to work was like play. We children tagged around with our elders and copied what they did. We followed our fathers to the fields and helped plant and weed. The old men took us for walks and taught us the use of plants and how to collect them. We joined the women in gathering rabbitweed for baskets and went with them to dig clay for pots. We would taste this clay as the women did to test it. We watched the fields to drive out the birds and rodents, helped pick peaches to dry in the sun and gather melons to lug up the mesa. We rode the burros to harvest corn, gather fuel, or herd sheep. In house-building we helped a little by bringing up dirt to cover the roofs. In this way we grew up doing things. All the old people said that it was a disgrace to be idle and that a lazy boy should be whipped.

**Don Talayesva** *Sun Chief*
Hopi *Hópitu*

born 1890, speaking c. 1938

# PLANT SOMETHING TO BE YOUR OWN

Well, when I was nine years old, I was able to help my mother. It was in spring when planting was begun that I was told, "Plant something to be your own." Sure enough, I did some planting. When they began to hoe weeds where it was planted, I was told, "Say! You weed in your field." My hoe was a little hoe. And soon the hoeing would cease. I was glad.

When we ceased bothering where it was planted, I was unwilling to do anything. But when I would be told, "When you finish this, then you may go and play with the little girls," I was willing. I then surely played violently with the children. We played tag, as we enjoyed it.

And at the time when what we planted was mature, I was told, "Say! You must try to cook what you have raised." Surely then I tried to cook. After I cooked it, my parents tasted it. "What she has raised tastes very well," they said to me. "And she has cooked it very carefully," I would be told. I was proud when they said that to me. As a matter of fact I was just told so that I might be encouraged to cook. And I thought, "It's probably true."


Anonymous woman
FOX   *Mĕshkwa Kihŭg*

born c. 1875, speaking in 1918


Joseph Kossuth Dixon *Stirring the pot* c. 1913

# THE SNAKE

Once I was out herding with four Paiute children, three girls and a boy, and we took the herd up in the canyon. There were lots of lakes

up in this canyon, and around them were all different kinds of brushes and weeds and lots of flag. Something sweet grows on the end of this flag, and we got into the brush for these sweet things. We took them off and ate them. After a while the girls went away, and the boy, too, and I was all alone there in the brush at the edge of the lake. When I started to go, there was a snake lying in front of me. I started back, I went back a little way trying to get out of the brush, and there was another. Then I called the Paiute children. The boy came, and I said, "There's a snake." There was nothing around, no sticks or stones, and when we'd try to get out one way, a snake would be lying there. Soon they were all around us. We called for the girls, but they were away, and we started crying. We were afraid of the snakes.

We were standing there, crying, and at last the girls came. The boy spoke to them—I don't know what he said, but I guess he called for some rocks and sticks—and they began throwing them to us. But the rocks didn't reach us; they dropped into the water, and so did the sticks. They couldn't throw them far enough. He must have wanted them to come for us, but they shook their heads and said, "No." One of us would start crying and then the other, and soon we were out of voice. We'd been standing in the water all afternoon until the sun was pretty well down, when, as we started toward one place, nothing was there. We kept on moving along, holding each other, until at last we were out of the brush and water. We were so hungry, and we were voiceless, too, from crying.

Left Handed
NAVAJO  *Diné*

born 1868, speaking in 1934

John K. Hillers *Paiute girl and boy* Paiute 1873

# TREATED LIKE A SLAVE

From the time we moved from Colorada when I was four years old until I started work as a man when I was thirteen years old in Arizona, I was treated like a slave in the family. I had to find grass for our burros every day. Whenever there was an errand, I was sent. If I was sent to the store two miles away, *mama grande* would spit on the floor as I left, telling me that if I was not back before the spit dried she would beat me. For several months we bought bread from a Mexican who lived south of the river. He passed a half mile from our house about four o'clock in the morning on his way into Hermosillo. I was the one who had to get up and go wait for him in the cold without a coat. I was given the oldest, thinnest blankets and was cold all winter. My *mama grande* was friendly to everyone else and she had been nice to me in Colorada, but she became my bitter enemy in Hermosillo. My aunt Camilda had never paid any attention to me in Colorada, but at La Playita I had to go to town with her all the time. She got mad at me every day, and she used to chase me through the orchard because she wanted to beat me; she could never run fast enough to catch me. When she got really mad at me, she would say I was going to turn into a witch.

Rosalio Moisés
YAQUI

1869–1969, writing c. 1954

John K. Hillers *Paiute woman and children* Paiute 1873

# BURIED ALIVE

Oh, what a fright we all got one morning to hear some white people were coming. Everyone ran as best they could. My poor mother was left with my little sister and me. Oh, I never can forget it. My poor mother was carrying my little sister on her back, and trying to make me run; but I was so frightened I could not move my feet, and while my poor mother was trying to get me along, my aunt overtook us, and she said to my mother: "Let us bury our girls, or we shall all be killed and eaten up." So they went to work and buried us, and told us if we heard any noise not to cry out, for if we did they would surely kill us and eat us. So our mothers buried me and my cousin, planted sage bushes over our faces to keep the sun from burning them, and there we were left all day.

Oh, can anyone imagine my feelings *buried alive,* thinking every minute that I was to be unburied and eaten up by the people that my grandfather loved so much? With my heart throbbing, and not daring to breathe, we lay there all day. It seemed that the night would never come.

Thanks be to God! the night came at last. Oh, how I cried and said, "Oh, father, have you forgotten me? Are you never coming for me?" I cried so I thought my very heartstrings would break.

At last we heard some whispering. We did not dare to whisper to each other, so we lay still. I could hear their footsteps coming nearer and nearer. I thought my heart was coming right out of my mouth. Then I heard my mother say, "It is right here!" Oh, can anyone in this world ever imagine what were my feelings when I was dug up by my poor mother and father? My cousin and I were once more happy in our mothers' and fathers' care, and we were taken to where all the rest were.

I was once buried alive. But my second burial shall be forever, where no father or mother will come and dig me up. It shall not be with throbbing heart that I shall listen for coming footsteps. I shall be in the sweet rest of peace—I, the chieftain's weary daughter.

Well, while we were in the mountains hiding, the people that my grandfather called our white brothers came along to where our winter supplies were. They set everything we had left on fire. It was a fearful sight. It was all we had for the winter, and it was all burnt during that night. My father took some of his men during the night to try and save some of it, but they could not; it had burnt down before they got there.


Sarah Winnemucca Hopkins
PAIUTE  *Numu*

c. 1844–1891, writing c. 1882


56

# MY NEW LIFE

Thirty miles from the school I met Dr. Riggs on the road, coming to the town of Yankton, and received some encouraging words from him, for he spoke the Sioux language very well. A little further on I met the Indian agent, Major Sears, a Quaker, and he, too, gave me a word of encouragement when he learned that I had walked a hundred and fifty miles to school. My older brother John, who was then assistant teacher and studying under Dr. Riggs, met me at the school and introduced me to my new life.

The bell of the old chapel at Santee summoned the pupils to class. Our principal read aloud from a large book and offered prayer. Although he conducted devotional exercises in the Sioux language, the subject matter was still strange, and the names he used were unintelligible to me. "Jesus" and "Jehovah" fell upon my ears as mere meaningless sounds.

I understood that he was praying to the "Great Mystery" that the work of the day might be blessed and their labor be fruitful. A cold sweat came out upon me as I heard him ask the "Great Mystery" to be with us in that day's work in that school building. I thought it was too much to ask of Him. I had been taught that the Supreme Being is only concerned with spirits, and that when one wishes to commune with Him in nature he must be in a spiritual attitude and must retire from human sound or influence, alone in the wilderness. Here for the first time I heard Him addressed openly in the presence of a house full of young men and young girls!

**Charles A. Eastman**   *Obiyesa*
WAHPETON SIOUX   *Dakota*

1858–1939, writing c. 1916

# A WHITE MAN'S NAME

One day when we came to school, there was a lot of writing on one of the blackboards. We did not know what it meant, but our interpreter came into the room and said, "Do you see all these marks on the blackboard? Well, each word is a white man's name.

They are going to give each one of you one of these names by which you will hereafter be known." None of the names were read or explained to us, so of course we did not know the sound or meaning of any of them.

The teacher had a long pointed stick in her hand, and the interpreter told the boy in the front seat to come up. The teacher handed the stick to him, and the interpreter then told him to pick out any name he wanted. The boy had gone up with his blanket on. When the long stick was handed to him, he turned to us as much as to say, "Shall I—or will you help me to—take one of these names? Is it right for me to take a white man's name?" He did not know what to do for a time, not uttering a single word—but he acted a lot and was doing a lot of thinking.

Finally he pointed out one of the names written on the blackboard. Then the teacher took a piece of white tape and wrote the name on it. Then she cut off a length of the tape and sewed it on the back of the boy's shirt. Then that name was erased from the board. There was no duplication of names in the first class at Carlisle School!

Then the next boy took the pointer and selected a name. He was also labeled in the same manner as Number One. When my turn came, I took the pointer and acted as if I were about to touch an enemy. Soon we all had the names of white men sewed on our backs.


Luther Standing Bear    *Mato Najin*
Brulé Sioux    *Lakota*

1868–1939, writing c. 1928


Anon. *Math class at the Carlisle School*  1903

# THE CUTTING OF MY LONG HAIR

Late in the morning, my friend Judéwin gave me a terrible warning. Judéwin knew a few words of English, and she had overheard the paleface woman talk about cutting our long, heavy hair. Our mothers had taught us that only unskilled warriors who were captured had their hair shingled by the enemy. Among our people, short hair was worn by mourners, and shingled hair by cowards!

John Nicholas Choate *Chiricahua Apaches as they arrived at the Carlisle School* Apache 1886

We discussed our fate some moments, and when Judéwin said, "We have to submit, because they are strong," I rebelled.

"No, I will not submit! I will struggle first!" I answered.

I watched my chance, and when no one noticed, I disappeared. I crept up the stairs as quietly as I could in my squeaking shoes—my moccasins had been exchanged for shoes. Along the hall I passed, without knowing whither I was going. Turning aside to an open door, I found a large room with three white beds in it. The windows were

John Nicholas Choate *The same group two months later* Apache 1886

covered with dark green curtains, which made the room very dim. Thankful that no one was there, I directed my steps toward the corner farthest from the door. On my hands and knees I crawled under the bed, and cuddled myself in the dark corner.

From my hiding place I peered out, shuddering with fear whenever I heard footsteps nearby. Though in the hall loud voices were calling my name, and I knew that even Judéwin was searching for me, I did not open my mouth to answer. Then the steps were quickened and the voices became excited. The sounds came nearer and nearer. Women and girls entered the room. I held my breath and watched them open closet doors and peep behind large trunks. Someone threw up the curtains, and the room was filled with sudden light. What caused them to stoop and look under the bed I do not know. I remember being dragged out, though I resisted by kicking and scratching wildly. In spite of myself, I was carried downstairs and tied fast in a chair.

I cried aloud, shaking my head all the while until I felt the cold blades of the scissors against my neck, and heard them gnaw off one of my thick braids. Then I lost my spirit. Since the day I was taken from my mother I had suffered extreme indignities. People had stared at me. I had been tossed about in the air like a wooden puppet. And now my long hair was shingled like a coward's! In my anguish I moaned for my mother, but no one came to comfort me. Not a soul reasoned quietly with me, as my own mother used to do; for now I was only one of many little animals driven by a herder.


Gertrude Bonnin    *Zitkala-Ṡa*
Yankton Sioux    *Nakota*

1878–1938, writing in 1899

62

# I WANTED TO GO HOME

When I got back to Carlisle, it was during vacation time, and most of the students had gone out to work. There was no school, and there were no studies. This was not the life I desired, and I became lonesome. Finally I told Captain Pratt I wanted to go home to my people. He objected.

"No, Luther," he said, "I want you to stay here. When school is open again, you may go to school a whole day instead of a half day, or you can take care of the wardrobe half a day if you prefer."

But I said: "No, I want to go home, but I want to go in the right way. Several of the boys have run away from you, but I do not want to do that."

"All right," said Captain Pratt. "You may go, but I want you to promise that you will come back."

I answered that if I cared to come back I would do so.

Captain Pratt wrote a letter to the agent at Rosebud Agency. Then he gave me money for my ticket and five dollars extra for meals. I had some money of my own in addition.

So I said farewell to the school life and started back to my people, but with a better understanding of life. There would be no more hunting—we would have to work now for our food and clothing. It was like the Garden of Eden after the fall of man.

**Luther Standing Bear**  *Mato Najin*
Brulé Sioux  *Lakota*

1868–1939, writing c. 1928

# I KNEW THE NAMES OF THE PLANTS AND TREES

When I was about ten or twelve years old, I knew the names of the common plants and trees, because I had gone around with other boys and listened to older people talk about them. At the same age I knew the name of almost every bird, because we boys used to hunt them all the time. We knew about animals also. When traveling, if we crossed an animal's track, our parents would point it out and say, "That is a deer track" or "That is a bear track." But it was not until I was fifteen years old or so, and had started hunting with my older sister's husband and a maternal uncle, that I really began to learn how these birds, animals, and plants were related. My maternal uncle, an old man, taught me all the different names of plants and animals and how they were related. For instance, while we hunted, he told me that jackrabbits and cottontails were relatives; that chipmunk and rock squirrel were relatives. This is how I learned. By the time I was twenty I knew all these things about animals and plants. I learned later on how our people believe that the wind comes in the spring and shakes the trees to life. We have a word for this, and I can remember, after I was married, hearing older people talk about it and wondering what the word meant. Shortly after that, I found out.

John Rope
WESTERN WHITE MOUNTAIN APACHE  *Inde*

speaking c. 1930

John Alvin Anderson *A Brulé woman and child* Sioux c. 1880s

65

# TWO BOYS

I learned to hunt when I was just a young boy. I made all my own
bows and arrows, and hunted in the valley for rabbits and ducks.
I picked up this knowledge of hunting partly from the boys who
always knew something about it and partly from my father's
teachings. . . .

When I was still a little older, I dreamed that my soul said to me:
"Now I am a young man. I will go hunting and kill all the animals."
I also dreamed that I had made bows and arrows and that I had
painted the arrowshafts blue where the feathers are and red a little
way in front of this. I made my arrows afterward, as I had done in the
dream. I got the blue from a growth on rabbit brush. These colors are
not for magic. They are just to make the arrows look well. The same
night I dreamed that I took an eagle wing and placed it across the
back of my head, and my soul said: "I will go hunting high up in the
Sierra Nevada as an eagle does. I will not be hindered by obstacles,
but will be able to go over everything." Afterward, I became a great
hunter. I could stand long and tiring trips through the mountains and
could cross the roughest country. . . .

When I was still a young man, I saw Birch Mountain in a dream.
It said to me: "You will always be well and strong. Nothing can hurt
you, and you will live to an old age." After this, Birch Mountain came
and spoke to me whenever I was in trouble and told me that I would
be all right. That is why nothing has happened to me and why I am
so old now.

Jack Stewart
OWENS VALLEY PAIUTE   *Numu*

born c. 1837, speaking c. 1927

A. Frank Randall *Apache hunters*
Apache 1888

When I was a young boy, I knew nothing about hunting, so I did not try it often. I guess the reason was that my father died when I was very young, and neither my uncle nor other relatives took the responsibility of teaching me. I never did dream of a power. I played games with the boys sometimes but had very little success. When we played throwing arrows at a hoop, I generally lost all my arrows; for in the first place I did not know how to make good arrows and in the second place I could not throw them. But the honor of our family was upheld in these things by my cousin, Yärovü′gavü′ü, who made good arrows and always won. Whenever I played games of throwing or shooting at targets, I simply lost my arrows.

Sam Newland
OWENS VALLEY PAIUTE *Numu*

born c. 1840, speaking c. 1927

67

# THE POWER OF A BIRD

Old Lady Yube died quite a while back. One day I was at her camp at Rinconada. I used to stay with these people. I was a little boy, but old enough to know things. I was lying in the shade. A cedar waxwing was coming toward me. I was just about to shoot it when she looked up (she was weaving a basket) and said, "Don't shoot!" I put down my arrows.

The bird stayed there and sang. She said, "I hope it means nothing but good." It looked like she was talking to that bird. She said, "Don't say anything against that bird. It's coming to help me, to help me make baskets and to sell my baskets, and to tell me about the herbs and about the bites of animals and how to cure them."

"Can I shoot these birds?"

"No, do not shoot them. Shoot any other birds but these."

She said to me, "That bird is good in many ways. Good birds like these we should not bother. To shoot birds that we have no use for is no good. They sing around camp. If you are sad and don't feel well, when they sing you feel better." She put her basket away and spoke to me, and I listened. "Life-Giver sends us these birds. They tell us many things. They are too small to use. So it's best to leave them alone. It's just like you, now. Suppose that you were small and the bird was large and it came for you and wanted to eat you. How would you like it?"

"Oh, I wouldn't let any bird eat me. I'd kill it."

"No, I'm telling you this for a lesson, to show you that you should leave birds alone."

The only toothache I had was right there. It happened to me right where she spoke to me that time. I couldn't stop crying. She said, "Now, watch and that bird will come."

I was wishing and wishing that it would come. It didn't come all day. Then it came. I looked at me and was afraid to light. I said,

"Bird, I'm sick; I can't hurt you." The bird sat there and sang.

Then the old woman came out. She heard it singing. She talked to it, and it sang on the palm of her hand. She spoke to it, and it took something out of its mouth and put it in her hand. She took it and rubbed it all over my jaw where it was sore. It was sticky and felt good. It felt as if the pain was all being pulled out. That night I slept soundly, and the next day the swelling was down. She did this four times, and then my toothache disappeared. I didn't go to the doctor at all. When she did it, she sang songs and the bird sang also.

Chris

CHIRICAHUA APACHE/MESCALERO APACHE  *Inde*

born c. 1880, speaking c. 1935

# THE GOD OF THE WINDS

I will now relate what I dreamed when I was but twelve years old, and also my father's interpretation of my dream.

Myself and others were sleeping far from the wigwam, near a large pine. I saw, in my dream, a person coming from the east; he approached, walking on the air. He looked down upon me and said, "Is this where you are?" I said, "Yes." "Do you see this pine?" "Yes, I see it." "It is a great and high tree." I observed that the tree was lofty, reaching toward the heavens—its branches extended over land and water, and its roots were very deep.

"Look on it while I sing; yes, gaze upon the tree." He sang and pointed to the tree. It commenced waving its top, the earth about its roots was heaved up, and the waters roared and tossed from one side of their beds to the other. As soon as he stopped singing and let fall his hands, everything became perfectly still and quiet. "Now," said he, "sing the words which I have sung." I commenced as follows—

It is I who travel in the winds,
It is I who whisper in the breeze;
I shake the trees,
I shake the earth,
I trouble the waters on every land.

While singing, I heard the winds whistle, saw the tree waving its top, the earth heaving, heard the waters roaring, because they were all troubled and agitated. Then said he, "I am from the rising of the sun; I will come and see you again. You will not see me often, but you will hear me speak." Thus spoke the spirit and then turned away toward the road from which he had come.

I told my father of my dream, and after hearing all, he said, "My son, the god of the winds is kind to you. The aged tree, I hope, may indicate long life; the wind may indicate that you will travel much; the water which you saw, and the winds, will carry your canoe safely through the waves."

George Copway  *Kah-ge-ga-gah-bowh*
CHIPPEWA  *Ojibwa*

born 1818, writing in 1850

# A FAST

So there I fasted, at the black hawk's nest where a lodge had been built for me. The first night I stayed there I wondered when things would happen; but nothing took place. The second night, rather late in the night, my father came and opened the war bundle and, taking a gourd out, began to sing. I stood beside him without any clothing on me except the breechcloth, and holding tobacco in each hand, I uttered my cry to the spirits as my father sang. He sang war bundle songs, and he wept as he sang. I also wept as I uttered my cry to the spirits. When he was finished, he told me some sacred stories and then went home.

When I found myself alone, I began to think that something ought to happen to me soon, yet nothing occurred, so I had to pass another day there. On the third night I was still there. My father visited me again, and we repeated what we had done the night before. In the morning, just before sunrise, I uttered my cry to the spirits. The fourth night found me still there. Again my father came and we did the same things, but in spite of it all, I experienced nothing unusual. Soon another day dawned upon us. That morning I told my elder brother that I had been blessed by spirits and that I was going home to eat. However, I was not telling the truth. I was hungry, and I also knew that on the following night we were going to have a feast and that I would have to utter my cry to the spirits again. I dreaded that. So I went home. When I got there, I told my people the story I had told my brother—that I had been blessed and that the spirits had told me to eat. I was not speaking the truth, yet they gave me the food that is carefully prepared for those who have been blessed.

Sam Blowsnake  *Big Winnebago*
WINNEBAGO  *Hotcangara*

born c. 1875, writing c. 1917

# A VISION

It was four years old then, and I think it must have been the next summer that I first heard the voices. It was a happy summer and nothing was afraid, because in the Moon When the Ponies Shed (May) word came from the Wasichus that there would be peace and that they would not use the road anymore and that all the soldiers would go away. The soldiers did go away and their towns were torn down; and in the Moon of Falling Leaves (November) they made a treaty with Red Cloud that said our country would be ours as long as grass should grow and water flow. You can see that it is not the grass and the water that have forgotten.

Maybe it was not this summer when I first heard the voices, but I think it was, because I know it was before I played with bows and arrows or rode a horse, and I was out playing alone when I heard them. It was like somebody calling me, and I thought it was my mother, but there was nobody there. This happened more than once and always made me afraid, so that I ran home.

It was when I was five years old that my grandfather made me a bow and some arrows. The grass was young and I was on horseback. A thunderstorm was coming from where the sun goes down, and just as I was riding into the woods along a creek, there was a kingbird sitting on a limb. This was not a dream, it happened. And I was going to shoot at the kingbird with the bow my grandfather made when the bird spoke and said: "The clouds all over are one-sided." Perhaps it meant that all the clouds were looking at me. And then it said: "Listen! A voice is calling you!" Then I looked up at the clouds, and two men were coming there, headfirst, like arrows slanting down; and as they came, they sang a sacred song and the thunder was like drumming. I will sing it for you. The song and the drumming were like this:

Elliott and Fry *Black Elk (left)
and Yellow Hand (right)* Sioux 1887

Behold, a sacred voice is calling you,
All over the sky a sacred voice is calling.

I sat there gazing at them, and they were coming from the place where the giant lives (north). But when they were very close to me, they wheeled about toward where the sun goes down, and suddenly they were geese. Then they were gone, and the rain came with a big wind and a roaring.

I did not tell this vision to anyone. I liked to think about it, but I was afraid to tell it.

**Black Elk** *Hehaka Sapa*
OGLALA SIOUX *Lakota*

1863–1950, speaking in 1931

# EVERYTHING IS OVERFLOWING

That night he came, and they started on the songs. After Who Has Mules was through repeating all the songs and all the prayers that go with them and all the stories about them, the stories about the sheep, horses, properties, and other things, my father said, "Now you've learned everything. You remember everything from where we started to where we stopped. Now I know you remember things, and I think you're a smart man. There are lots of people who can't learn these songs, and now you've learned a few of them. When you start using them on your stocks and properties, if you do it right, you'll soon have everything. Now you can go ahead. You wanted to learn, and I told you you could. I promised you, and I've given it to you."

He cupped his hands and spread them out before him and said, "You see, you think there's nothing in my hands, but my hands are full. Everything is overflowing, things are falling out of my hands. That's the way you'll be later on. So just stick to it and learn some more if you want to.

"You must remember everything I've said to you. I told you that I had a handful of things and that you'd be that way sometime, but you'll have to have a hard time first. You won't get this way just as soon as you learn all the songs about them. You have to work for all these things. You have to go through many dangerous places, down in the arroyos, in the canyons, and climb up and down mountains. You have to kick sticks and rocks and get splinters in your feet and hands and be cut. You may think you'll get them all as soon as you learn the songs, but you must suffer a great deal before you get them. After you've suffered, then, for all your knowing you'll have a handful of things, and you'll look at them and won't know what to do with them. But you'll use them all the time. After you get all this stuff, your children will have everything. They won't starve, they won't be ragged, they won't hunger for meat and other things. They'll have everything, if you have it on hand for them. And you can help the poor and others with it all the time. That's after you get all these things, but before that you must be stingy."

They were up all night. Early in the morning my father said, "Now you've learned all that I know, all the songs, prayers, and stories. I wanted you to learn, for you are my only nephew. I know you wish to have lots of stock and property, and I know you need them, I know you have children. I don't want your children to go starving. So, now you can go ahead, tend to your stocks and properties, and do it right. And don't talk roughly, because you've learned many songs and prayers. If you know the songs and prayers, you don't want to talk roughly. If you do, you won't get these things, because all the stocks and properties will know that you'll be rough with them. They'll be afraid and won't want to come to you. If you think kindly and talk in the kindest manner, then they'll know you're a kind man, and then everything will go to you. So, now, just go ahead, this is all I want to say to you. This will be the end." That's what my father said, and Who Has Mules went home.

Left Handed

NAVAJO *Diné*

born 1868, speaking in 1934

# AFTER THE EVENING MEAL

After the evening meal was over, everything was put away. Then my grandfather would start his stories just like I'm doing now. As soon as he started his stories, we couldn't run around. There were lots of us children. We were asked to sit and listen. There would be no noise, you could hear nothing but the storyteller.

Now, where the children are—they never listen to whoever is speaking. They are all very noisy. We were never like that. I don't blame them. They don't understand when I'm speaking among them in my own language. That's the way I look at it. But at that time we understood our language and what was being said, so we listened. The next morning we would go through the same thing, and again the evening stories would begin. Now children go to school, but that's the way it was with us. I never knew a time that an evening was missed on telling history or stories.

When my grandfather would go through all the story about our living from life way back, then he would tell us, *"Haaw, yee een áyá ak kwatlaakw ax dachxanx'i sáani"* (I will tell you fairy tales, my grandchildren). Then he would start the stories about Raven. You people call it fairy tales, we call it *tlaagú*.

He would then start right from the beginning, when Raven came down among the people of the dark. This is where it would begin. Raven didn't know yet, at that time, that he made the world. Where is daylight? Where will he find it? He didn't know where it was.

**Charlie Joseph, Sr.** *Kaal.átk'*
Tlingit *Kaagwaantaan*

1895–1986, speaking in 1978

Anon. *Sitka Jake in a chilkat dance blanket* Tlingit c. 1900

76

# INDEX OF SPEAKERS AND WRITERS

In the main text, speakers and writers have been identified by the name by which they are best known in **bold type**, accompanied where applicable by their name in their own language or a translation of it, in *italics*. Only the first of these names is listed here. In transliterating names, I have retained the forms given in the source texts. Some names—such as Chris, Mourning Dove, and Jim Whitewolf—are pseudonyms. Readers should note that Sam Blowsnake is often referred to by the name Crashing Thunder, the title of his autobiography; this was actually the name of his brother, Jasper Blowsnake, transferred to Sam by the anthropologist Paul Radin, who feared that Sam's own name, Big Winnebago, might seem unintentionally amusing.

# INDEX OF INDIAN NATIONS

The Indian nations are identified first by their common name, accompanied where possible by their own name for themselves. So the PAPAGO ("Bean People") are also the *Tohono O'odham* ("People of the Sunlight" or "Desert People"). Readers should note that many of the common names for Indian nations are taken from names first given to them by their enemies and may contain derogatory implications. Most of the preferred names simply signify "The People." Only the common names are listed below.

# FURTHER READING

Bataille, Gretchen M., and Kathleen Mullen Sands. *American Indian Women: Telling Their Lives*. Lincoln and London: University of Nebraska Press, 1984.

Bruchac, Joseph. *Lasting Echoes: An Oral History of Native American People*. San Diego, New York, and London: Silver Whistle, 1997.

Brumble, H. David. *An Annotated Bibliography of American Indian and Eskimo Autobiographies*. Lincoln and London: University of Nebraska Press, 1981.

————. *American Indian Autobiography*. Berkeley, Los Angeles, and London: University of California Press, 1988.

Griffin-Pierce, Trudy. *The Encyclopedia of Native America*. New York: Viking, 1995.

Hilger, M. Inez. *Chippewa Child Life and Its Cultural Background*. St. Paul: Minnesota Historical Society Press, 1992 (first published 1951).

Katz, Jane. *Messengers of the Wind: Native American Women Tell Their Life Stories*. New York: Ballantine Books, 1995.

Krupat, Arnold. *Native American Autobiography: An Anthology*. Madison, Wisconsin: University of Wisconsin Press, 1994.

Leighton, Dorothea, and Clyde Kluckhohn. *Children of the People: The Navaho Individual and His Development*. Cambridge: Harvard University Press, 1947.

Miller, Lee. *From the Heart: Voices of the American Indian*. New York: Alfred A. Knopf, 1995.

Opler, Morris Edward. *Childhood and Youth in Jicarilla Apache Society*. Los Angeles: The Southwest Museum, 1946.

Riley, Patricia. *Growing Up Native American*. New York: William Morrow and Company, 1993.

Swanton, John R. *The Indian Tribes of North America*. Washington and London: Smithsonian Institution Press, 1969 (first published 1952).

# PICTURE SOURCES

Grateful acknowledgment is made to the following institutions for permission to reproduce photographs, with special thanks to Paula Richardson Fleming at the Smithsonian Institution, National Anthropological Archives.

**Alaska State Library, Historical Collections** 23 (neg. PCA 57-140); **The British Library** endpapers (shelfmark L. R. 298. a. 32); **Guildhall Library, Corporation of London** half-title, 3, 7, 9, 12, 16, 21, 33, 37 (all from Edward S. Curtis *The North American Indian*, 1907-1930); **Library of Congress, Prints and Photographs Division** 39 (neg. LC-US262-101159), 44 (LC-US262-86438), 58 (LC-US262-72450); **Nebraska State Historical Society** 30 (neg. A547:1-88), 54 (neg. A547:2-228); **New York Public Library, Miriam and Ira D. Wallach Division of Art, Prints & Photographs, Astor, Lenox and Tilden Foundations** iv (neg. 81-799); **Royal British Columbia Museum, Victoria, British Columbia** 41 (neg. PN 1869); **Smithsonian Institution, National Anthropological Archives** 10 (neg. 556,388), 15 (92-13,271), 24 (neg. 4604), 27 (neg. 2751), 42 (neg. 53,340-C), 48 (neg. 1807-A), 50 (neg. 83-7850), 52 (neg. 1632), 55 (neg. 1599), 60 (neg. 52,542), 61 (neg. 52,543), 67 (neg. 2491-A), 73 (neg. 72-7016), 76 (neg. 56,769); **University of Nevada–Reno Library, Lorenzo Creel Collection, Special Collections** opposite title page (neg. 2710/810).

# TEXT SOURCES AND ACKNOWLEDGMENTS

Grateful acknowledgment is made to the following sources and copyright holders. Every effort has been made to trace the owners of copyright, and we apologize for any omissions.

**Anonymous man**. "The Old Man" and "This Is Your Camp," from Morris Edward Opler, *An Apache Life-Way: The Economic, Social, and Religious Institutions of the Chiricahua Indians* (Lincoln and London: University of Nebraska Press, 1996; first published Chicago: University of Chicago Press, 1941), copyright 1941 by the University of Chicago Press. Reprinted by permission of the University of Nebraska Press.

**Anonymous woman**. "Plant Something to Be Your Own," from Truman Michelson, "The Autobiography of a Fox Indian Woman" (Fortieth Annual Report of the Bureau of American Ethnology, 1918–19, Washington: Government Printing Office, 1925).

**Black Elk**. "A Vision" and "Playing War," from John G. Neihardt, *Black Elk Speaks* (New York: Morrow, 1932) copyright 1932, 1959, 1972 by John G. Neihardt, copyright © 1961 by the John G. Neihardt Trust. Reprinted by permission of the University of Nebraska Press.

**Blowsnake, Sam**. "A Fast" and "Crying to the Spirits," from Paul Radin, *The Autobiography of a Winnebago Indian* (University of California Publications in American Archaeology and Ethnology, vol. 16, no. 7, Berkeley: University of California Press, 1920; later expanded as *Crashing Thunder*, New York: Appleton and Company, 1926).

**Bonnin, Gertrude (Zitkala-Ša)**. "I Was a Wild Little Girl" and "The Cutting of My Long Hair," from Zitkala-Ša, "Impressions of an Indian Childhood" (*Atlantic Monthly*, 1900; collected in *American Indian Stories*, Glorieta, New Mexico: Rio Grande Press, 1976).

**Chona, Maria**. "Ah, How We Could Run" and "Morning-Stands-Up," from Ruth M. Underhill, *The Autobiography of a Papago Woman* (Memoirs of the American Anthropological Association, no. 46, 1936; later expanded as *Papago Woman*, New York: Holt, Rinehart and Winston, 1979).

**Chris**. "The Power of a Bird," from Morris Edward Opler, *Apache Odyssey: A Journey Between Two Worlds* (New York: Holt, Rinehart and Winston, 1969), copyright © 1969 by Holt, Rinehart and Winston, Inc.

**Copway, George**. "The God of the Winds" and "The Great Spirit," from George Copway, *Recollections of a Forest Life: or, The Life and Travels of Kah-ge-ga-gah-bowh, or, George Copway, Chief of the Ojibway Nation* (London: C. Gilpin, 1850).

**Dutchman, Louise**. "How I Got My Name," from Leonard Bloomfield, *Menomini Texts* (New York: G. E. Stechert & Co., for the American Ethnological Society, 1928).

**Eastman, Charles A**. "An Indian Must Always Rise Early" from Charles A. Eastman, *Indian Boyhood* (Boston: Little, Brown and Co., 1922; first published 1902). "My New Life," from Charles A. Eastman, *From the Deep Woods to Civilization: Chapters in the Autobiography of an Indian* (Boston: Little, Brown and Co., 1916).

**Hopkins, Sarah Winnemucca**. "Buried Alive," from Sarah Winnemucca Hopkins, ed. Mrs. Horace Mann, *Life Among the Piutes: Their Wrongs and Claims* (New York: G. P. Putnam's Sons, 1883).

**Irwin, Louis Two Ravens**. "The World Around Us," from Louis Two Ravens Irwin and Robert Liebert, *Two Ravens: The Life and Teachings of a Spiritual Warrior* (Rochester, Vermont: Destiny Books, 1996), copyright © 1996 by Daphne Irwin and Robert M. Liebert.

**Joseph, Charlie**. "After the Evening Meal," from Nora Marks Dauenhauer and Richard Dauenhauer, *Haa Kusteeyí, Our Culture: Tlingit Life Stories* (Seattle and London: University of Washington Press; Juneau: Sealaska Heritage Foundation, 1994), copyright © 1994 by Sealaska Heritage Foundation. Reprinted by permission of Sealaska Heritage Foundation.

**Lame Deer (John Fire)**. "Things I Was Told Not to Do," from John Fire/Lame Deer and Richard Erdoes, *Lame Deer: Seeker of Visions* (New York: Simon and Schuster, 1972), copyright © 1972 by John Fire/Lame Deer and Richard Erdoes. Reprinted by permission of Simon & Schuster.

**Left Handed**. "Everything Is Overflowing," "Racing Under the Sun," and "The Snake," from *Left Handed, Son of Old Man Hat*, recorded by Walter Dyk (Lincoln: University of Nebraska Press, 1967; first published as *Son of Old Man Hat* by Harcourt, Brace, and World, 1938), copyright 1938 by Walter Dyk, copyright © renewed 1966 by Walter Dyk. Reprinted by permission of the University of Nebraska Press.

**Moisés, Rosalio**. "Treated Like a Slave," from Rosalio Moisés, Jane Holden Kelley, and William Curry Holden, *A Yaqui Life: The Personal Chronicle of a Yaqui Indian* (Lincoln and London: University of Nebraska Press, 1977; first published as *The Tall Candle*, 1971), copyright © 1971 by the University of Nebraska Press, copyright renewed 1999 by the University of Nebraska Press. Reprinted by permission of the University of Nebraska Press.

**Mourning Dove**. "Dolls Never Appealed to Me," from *Mourning Dove: A Salishan Autobiography*, edited by Jay Miller (Lincoln and London: University of Nebraska Press, 1990), copyright © 1990 by the University of Nebraska Press. Reprinted by permission of the University of Nebraska Press.

**Newland, Sam, and Jack Stewart**. "Two Boys," from Julian H. Steward, *Two Paiute Autobiographies* (University of California Publications in American Archaeology and Ethnology, vol. 33, no. 5, Berkeley: University of California Press, 1934).

**Nowell, Charles James**. "Marching Around," from Clellan S. Ford, *Smoke from Their Fires: The Life of a Kwakiutl Chief* (New Haven: Yale University Press for the Institute of Human Relations, 1941), copyright 1941 by Yale University Press. Reprinted by permission of Yale University Press.

**Plenty-coups**. "Learning to Run," from Frank B. Linderman, *Plenty-coups: Chief of the Crows* (Lincoln: University of Nebraska Press, 1962; first published as *American: The Life Story of a Great Indian*, New York: John Day Co., 1930), copyright 1930 by Frank B. Linderman, copyright © renewed 1957 by Norma Linderman Waller, Verne Linderman and Wilda Linderman. Reprinted by permission of HarperCollins Publishers, Inc.

**Pretty-shield**. "I Tried to Be Like My Mother," from Frank B. Linderman, *Pretty-shield: Medicine Woman of the Crows* (Lincoln and London: University of Nebraska Press, 1972; first published as *Red Mother*, New York: John Day Co., 1932), copyright 1932 by Frank B. Linderman, copyright renewed 1960 by Norma Waller, Verne Linderman and Wilda Linderman. Reprinted by permission of HarperCollins Publishers, Inc.

**Price, Anna, John Rope,** and **Mrs. Andrew Stanley**. "Early Morning Swims," "I Knew the Names of the Plants and Trees," and "We Played at Getting Married," from Grenville Goodwin, *The Social Organization of the Western Apache* (Chicago and Illinois: University of Chicago Press, 1942), copyright 1942 by the University of Chicago Press.

**Rope, John**. *See* Price, Anna.

**Sewid, James**. "Some of the Kids Would Tease Me," from James P. Spradley, *Guests Never Leave Hungry: The Autobiography of James Sewid, a Kwakiutl Indian* (New Haven and London: Yale University Press, 1969), copyright © 1969 by Yale University. Reprinted by permission of Yale University Press.

**Standing Bear, Luther**. "A White Man's Name" and "I Wanted to Go Home," from Luther Standing Bear, *My People the Sioux* (Boston: Houghton Mifflin Company, 1928).

**Stanley, Mrs. Andrew**. *See* Price, Anna.

**Stewart, Jack**. *See* Newland, Sam.

**Talayesva, Don**. "Learning to Work," from Leo W. Simmons, *Sun Chief: The Autobiography of a Hopi Indian* (New Haven: Yale University Press, 1942), copyright 1942 by Yale University Press, copyright © renewed 1970 by Leo Simmons. Reprinted by permission of Yale University Press.

**White Man Runs Him**. "When We Were Quite Small Boys," from Joseph Kossuth Dixon, *The Vanishing Race: The Last Great Indian Council* (Garden City: Doubleday, Page and Co., 1913).

**Whitewolf, Jim**. "My Grandfather," from Charles S. Brant, *The Autobiography of a Kiowa Apache Indian* (New York: Dover Publications, Inc., 1991; first published as *Jim Whitewolf*, Dover, 1961), copyright © 1969 by Charles S. Brant. Reprinted by permission of Dover Publications, Inc.

**Yava, Albert**. "We Had Lots of Games," from *Big Falling Snow: A Tewa-Hopi Indian's Life and History and Traditions of His People* by Albert Yava, edited and annotated by Harold Courlander (New York: Crown, 1978), copyright © 1978 by Harold Courlander. Reprinted by permission of the Emma Courlander Trust.

**Zuñi, Lina**. "We Were Very Poor," from Ruth L. Bunzel, *Zuñi Texts* (New York: G. E. Stechert & Co. for the American Ethnological Society, 1933).